Breaking the Silence

*A Daughter's Story of Narcissistic Abuse, Survival, and
Self-Reclamation*

Genevieve McPartlin-Bryant

"Some things break you so deeply, you become someone new. But sometimes, that's the beginning of becoming who you were always meant to be."

Dedication:

To my son,

You are the reason I began this healing journey.

Your light gave me the courage to break the cycle

—

So you'd never have to carry the weight I did.

To the children I have yet to meet,

I'm doing this work now

So you will grow up in a home full of safety,
softness, and truth.

You are already loved beyond measure.

And to my husband,

Thank you for teaching me that love isn't
supposed to hurt.

Your kindness, patience, and steady presence

Showed me what it means to be truly seen – and
loved anyway.

You are the proof that good men exist.

And the reminder that I am worthy of everything
I once thought I'd never have.

Acknowledgments:

First, to my son—
You are the heartbeat of this book.
Your existence gave me the reason to heal, to grow,
to become.
Everything I broke free from, I did for you.
Thank you for making me a mother,
and for showing me what unconditional love really
feels like.

To my husband—
You came into my life with gentleness, patience, and
the kind of love I didn't know was possible.
You held space for my healing without trying to fix it,
and you reminded me—every single day—that I was
worthy of peace.
Thank you for walking beside me through it all.

To my brother—
You were the only one in the world who walked
through all of this beside me.
We didn't always have the words,
but we carried the same weight.
Thank you for surviving with me.

To my grandparents—
Thank you for stepping in when you didn't have to.
For filling in the gaps that others left behind.
For loving me with consistency, without hesitation,
and without question.

So much of the stability I had, came from the way you quietly showed up.

To my mom—
You were my safety when the world didn't feel safe.
Thank you for showing up, even when it was hard.
You were the constant when everything else felt like chaos.

To the friends who saw me, believed me, and loved me anyway—
Thank you for being light in the darkest moments.
Your presence reminded me that I didn't have to do this alone.

To my therapist—
Thank you for helping me find the voice I thought I lost.
You gave me the tools to rewrite my story—and the courage to tell it.

And finally, to every survivor who picks up this book:
You are not alone.
You are not too much.
You are not broken.
This is your reminder that healing is possible—and your voice is worth everything.

This book is a work of nonfiction based on the author's personal experiences. Some names and identifying details have been changed to protect the privacy of individuals.

For permission requests, write to the publisher at:
gmcpbryant@gmail.com

Printed in the United States of America
ISBN: 9798315621560

First Edition
Cover design by: Genevieve McPartlin-Bryant

Table of Contents:

Daddy is Gone

(Written October 2015, Age 14)

I feel alone—
like no one hears my cries for help.

Daddy is gone.
He is gone.

Will I ever see him again?
Or has he been taken to the dark side?

I think of him
with every step I take,
with every breath I breathe—
hoping he'll remember me.

If he never returns,
he shall still be there.

Maybe not visibly,
maybe not spiritually…
but still,
he is there.

I can feel him.
He is a part of me.
And even the darkest demons
could never take that away.

I've got his eyes and hair.
I've got his smile and mouth.

But is that enough?
I ask myself.

Only if I believe
will he be there for me.
Only if I don't let the demon inside take over.

Is it all in my head?

No.
My brother feels it too.
We are in the same hardship.

We shall never separate—
for siblings stick together,
through good and bad.

Maybe this is just a bad part…
one that seems to last forever.

PART I:
THE WOUND

Chapter 1:

The Smile That Hid the Hurt

They say children are resilient. That they bounce back. That they don't remember the small details. But I remember everything.

I was just two years old when my parents divorced. By the time I was two and a half, they had already moved on. My father found someone new — someone who would soon become his wife by the time I was three and a half. And just like that, my world, which was already fragile, began to feel like something I was being pushed out of rather than nurtured within.

As a little girl, I didn't have the words to explain the hollow feeling that settled in my chest whenever I was around her — my father's new wife. But I knew what it meant. She was the woman my father chose over my brother and me. And she never let us forget it. She made it painfully clear that we were not wanted. She'd say it outright: "They're not mine. I never wanted kids." But she married a man with a three-year-old and a seven-year-old. What did that make us? Inconveniences? Reminders?

I'll never forget being fourteen — just a freshman in high school — when my dad's side of the family gifted my grandparents a professional photoshoot. My grandma, the queen of candid photos — even when we had our mouths full — was glowing. Everyone was dressed to match — color coordinated — ready to capture a perfect moment. We were going to take a big family photo, then individual family shots. When our turn came — my father, his wife, my brother, and me — the photographer, who was a friend of the family but didn't know us well, offered some direction: "*Place your hand on your mom's shoulder.*"

At fourteen, I understood the world didn't always account for split families. I knew better than to take offense. But before I could even move, her voice cut through the moment like a knife: "*Oh no, they're not mine. I never wanted kids.*"

And she said it with a laugh. Like it was some kind of joke. Like my brother and I weren't standing right there. My father said nothing.

That was the pattern. Every other weekend, we'd go to his house, but those weekends were rarely spent with him. Date nights and plans with his wife meant we were dropped off at my grandparents' house. At the time, it stung. But now, I look back with gratitude. My grandparents gave us a love that was warm, unconditional, and safe. A love that stood in for the one we were supposed to get.

But as a child, it was confusing. It felt like rejection in the smallest, most subtle ways. Every missed opportunity. Every "maybe next time." Every time he handed us off so he could spend more time with her. I didn't have the vocabulary for emotional neglect back then. I just knew it felt like being unwanted.

The final blow came when I was nine.

It was supposed to be a day of magic. Christmas. The day I still believed in Santa, still clung to the idea that wishes mattered. But that was the day my father moved away. Not only did he decide to leave the state – he left without even telling us himself. He made my mom break the news. And then, on Christmas Day, while most kids were tearing open gifts and basking in twinkling lights, he was boarding a plane to Texas to start a new life with her. Her family. Her dreams.

I still believed in magic. But that was the Christmas the magic disappeared. That's the day I stopped believing that my father would ever put us first.

I sat there with wrapping paper at my feet, wondering what I did wrong.

And he didn't even say goodbye.

It was the first time I realized that a person could disappear from your life without even needing to shut the door. He just…left. And the silence that followed was deafening.

For a while, he made the effort. Monthly visits back to Illinois. He stayed with his parents and saw us. But slowly, the visits stretched out – every other month, then every few months. Eventually, it was six months between visits, sometimes longer. He went from being a father to a familiar voice on the phone… usually calling from the sidelines of someone else's child's game.

Because that's what hurt most of all.

He didn't just leave. He chose to be a father to someone else's kids. His wife's niece and nephew. He cheered them on. Went to their games. Bragged about them. Meanwhile, I was singing in choir for ten years, from second grade through graduation. He showed up maybe twice. I was a national archery champion – featured in a magazine. He never once saw me compete.

It wasn't just the distance. It was the silence. The indifference. The way I could walk into his massive home and see only *one* photo of my brother and me — faded, old, tucked away like an afterthought. Meanwhile, the other children — *her family* — were plastered throughout the entire hallway.

And yet, I smiled. I smiled in those family pictures. I smiled when people asked about my dad. I smiled because it was easier than explaining the ache. Easier than being told to "let it go" or "be grateful you have a dad at all."

I learned to smile through the holidays spent without him. Through the concerts and competitions where I scanned the crowd, always hoping — just in case. I smiled through Father's Day card crafts and pretend phone calls. I smiled through being the kid who didn't talk about her dad, because talking about him meant admitting the truth: he didn't really show up.

The smile became a shield. A performance. And eventually, a habit.

But behind the smile was a little girl whose heart had been quietly breaking for years.

She smiled, though she knew the truth. Her heart just wasn't ready to break where her mind already had.

Chapter 2:

Daddy's Love Was Never Free

You can't shatter something that never had the chance to be solid. That's what my relationship with my father felt like – unstable, fractured from the start. His love came with conditions, and I never seemed to meet them.

My father's love wasn't a gift – it was a bargain. A contract with invisible strings. Every kind gesture, every dollar spent, came with a price tag I couldn't see until the debt was due. He "helped" when it made him feel like the hero. But help with expectations attached isn't love. It's control.

My father's love was never freely given. It was something to be earned – through silence, obedience, or making myself small enough to fit the version of a daughter he could tolerate. I learned early on that his approval came at a cost, and even then, it was temporary.

He wasn't the kind of dad who called just to say he missed me. And if he did, there was something underlying that he needed to get off his chest. If the phone rang, it was usually because someone reminded him that he should check in. His voice always felt distant, like it belonged to someone playing the part of a father rather than being one.

There were rules – unspoken ones. Don't speak too much. Don't cry – because that's weak. Don't make things inconvenient. Don't expect too much. Love was never offered in abundance. It was doled out in crumbs, and only when he felt like I had earned them.

The older I got, the more I noticed the imbalance. The way he'd gush over other people's children – kids who weren't his but got the version of him I always wanted. He showed up for them. Cheered them on. Made space for them in his life. In his heart. On his walls.

But for me? I was lucky to get a phone call on my birthday. I stopped expecting meaningful presents or cards. I stopped holding my breath on Christmas. I accepted the gifts of money because I knew he didn't know anything about me. He wouldn't be able to go to a store and pick out something I liked – because he didn't know. I learned how to protect myself by not expecting anything at all.

And yet, I still wanted him to choose me. I still wanted to be enough.

That's the cruel part of being a child with a parent who dangles love like a prize – you grow up believing that if you were just *better,* just *more,* maybe they'd finally see you. Finally stay. But no matter how high I climbed; how many times I tried to earn it… his love always felt just out of reach.

When I was seventeen, I made the biggest leap of my life. I left the only home I'd known and moved across the country – from Illinois to Texas – to be closer to him. I told myself it was for school, for opportunity… but deep down, I know what I was chasing. I wanted a father. I wanted to believe that this would finally be the version of the story where he showed up.

He paid for my tuition, my housing, my groceries. On paper, it looked like generosity. But in my heart, it felt like a trap – even then. I was being bought, not loved. I was performing gratitude, not receiving care. And still, I stayed. Because I wanted it to be real.

I lived in Austin, just two and a half hours from him. Still, he didn't visit much. I had to go to him. He called sometimes. He helped when I needed something – but the favors always came back around.

I was reminded constantly: of the money he spent, the sacrifices he made, the *debt* I owed for his so-called kindness.

And then, things got worse. I ended up in a relationship that was everything love should never be – abusive, violent, manipulative. Physical, sexual, emotional. I was only a teenager, trying to piece together a life with no guide on what healthy love was supposed to look like. Sometimes I wonder if my father taught me – without meaning to – that love was supposed to hurt, or at least come with consequences.

Eventually, I broke. I needed safety. I needed my mom. I needed real family. So I made the choice to leave Texas and come back to Illinois, even though it meant starting over. And what did my father say? That since I "ran away," he wouldn't be helping with school anymore. His words cut deeper than any breakup every could.

"Your grandparents can pay for it," he told me, referring to my mom's parents. *"They did it for your brother."*

He didn't acknowledge why I left. I didn't feel safe enough to tell him. He didn't ask about my safety. He didn't try to understand the pain behind my decision. He just saw it as betrayal – as if love were a contract I'd broken.

The same grandparents he spoke about so casually had been the ones quietly covering for him for years. They were the ones who stepped up when he didn't. They were the ones who showed up without demanding anything in return.

And still, he held on to this twisted narrative: *I did so much for you, and you weren't even grateful.*

He reminded me of the car he helped me get in Texas. Brought it up every time we argued, like it gave him power over me. Like that one act of support canceled out a childhood of absence.

But what I would've given in that moment wasn't money. It wasn't groceries. It wasn't a car. I would've traded every dollar for a dad who stayed. For a dad who didn't make me feel like love had to be earned. For a dad who didn't disappear when I needed him most.

All I ever wanted was a father. A real one.

I didn't want to be bought — I wanted to be believed in. I wanted to matter, without owing anyone for it.

Chapter 3:

Growing Up Invisible

There's a kind of loneliness that has nothing to do with being alone. It's the kind that follows you into crowded rooms, loud dinner tables, and even family gatherings – especially family gatherings. It's the ache of being present but unseen. Not because you're hiding, but because no one is really looking.

That was my childhood. I existed in the background, like furniture. There, but not really acknowledged. A supporting role in someone else's story.

I was always unnoticed by my father. Even in comparison to my brother – four years older, easygoing, effortlessly smart. They were more like friends than father and son. My brother got straight A's without trying. I had to work for every decent grade I earned, and even then, it didn't feel like enough. Looking back, I know the emotional chaos I was living through didn't exactly help my focus in school.

I was labeled the "trouble child." Always grounded. Always "talking back." Always too emotional. My father didn't know how to handle me, and my mother could – but usually through consequence. The punishment was how I was managed, not understood.

Most of my weekends growing up were spent grounded. Fun was taken away like a reflex. But the truth was, all I really wanted was attention. Not attention in the loud or showy way – just to matter. Just to not feel like a burden, like the problem child who couldn't ever get it quite right.

I tried to be good. I really did. I knew my mom didn't need extra stress – she was a single mother, working hard at a job she loved, even if it didn't pay much. I saw how tired she was. So, I tried to be the child who didn't need anything. But my emotions always found a way to leak through the cracks.

That was the only time I was truly seen – when I broke. When I yelled, cried, or lost control. When my pain became too loud to ignore. And even then, I didn't get comfort. I got silence. Shut doors. Harsh words. Consequences. I was invisible until I made myself impossible to ignore – and then I was punished for it.

Being invisible when you're standing right in front of someone is one of the worst kinds of pain a child can experience.

No one checked in. No one asked why I was angry or sad or overwhelmed. They just called it drama. Mood swings. Attitude. But really? I just wanted to matter. I just wanted to be enough.

As an adult, I can see how all this shaped me into the woman I became – especially before I started to heal. I learned to hide my thoughts. I stayed quiet to avoid conflict. I became a people-pleaser. The "easy" one. I'd rather swallow my truth than risk being misunderstood.

I became soft-spoken, not because I was gentle – but because I believed my voice didn't deserve volume. I stayed quiet because I thought I was safer. I still do sometimes. I still hesitate to speak unless I feel completely sure of myself.

It sounds silly, but even trivia games are hard for me. I love them – really, I do. But if I don't know the answer with 100% certainty, I won't say anything. Not because I don't want to play, but because I'm scared of being wrong. Scared of being laughed at. Scared of disappointing the people around me.

It wasn't until I met my husband that I began to unlearn that fear. He reminds me – every day – that my voice matters. That I don't have to be perfect to be loved. That being wrong isn't the end of the world.

That I'm allowed to take up space.

Being unseen shaped me. Being loved anyway is what saved me.

Chapter 4:

The Lies We Tell to Survive

Sometimes, survival looks like pretending everything is okay.

We tell ourselves stories to soften the sharp edges. We make excuses for the people who hurt us. We smile through pain because the truth feels too heavy to carry in public.

I've told a lot of lies in my life – but not the kind you think. Not the kind meant to deceive. These were lies I told to survive.

"He does love me. He just doesn't know how to show it."

"I'm just being sensitive. It's not that deep."

"Maybe if I was better – quieter, smarter, easier – he would have stayed."

I told those stories until I believed them. Because telling the truth – that my father chose not to show up, that I wasn't a priority, that my pain didn't matter to him – was too much. So, I rewrote the narrative. I made him human. Flawed. "Busy." I said he did his best, even when I knew he didn't try at all.

I became the master of performing okay. Smiles in public, tears in silence. Straigtening my back when all I wanted to do was to fall apart. And when people asked if I was fine, I always said yes. Because if you repeat something enough, maybe it becomes real.

But it never did.

Sometimes, the lies we tell ourselves are the only way we can make sense of the people we love.

For years, I told myself that my stepmother was the reason he left. That she was the one who pulled him away, manipulated him, convinced him to choose a new life. And maybe she did play a role – her cruelty wasn't subtle. But the truth is, he was an adult. He made a choice. He chose *her*. And that thought destroyed me.

So, I told myself stories to cover the cracks.

"It's not his fault. She changed him."

"At least I have a home in Texas too."

But even that wasn't true. That "home" was more of an idea than a reality. I visited, sure – but I was more of a guest than a daughter. I didn't know where things were in the kitchen. I didn't know what drawer held the silverware. I didn't feel at ease there – I felt like I was borrowing space. So much so, that I packed loads of snacks in my suitcase when I visited – because it felt so wrong of me to go to the kitchen and look for something to eat when I was hungry.

And still, I held onto the lie. Because admitting the truth – that I didn't belong there, and maybe never really did – felt too big. Too painful.

I blamed myself constantly. Told myself *I* was the reason he left. That I was too emotional. Too dramatic. Too much work. That if I had just been easier to love, maybe he would've stayed. I even apologized to my brother once – told him I was sorry for making our dad leave. As if it were my fault. As if I had that kind of power.

Denial became my safety net – not just with my father, but with everyone who ever mistreated me. Even my abusers.

When I was fourteen, my virginity was stolen from me – violently, without consent. And when I tried to process the trauma, all I could hear was his voice:

"No one's going to want you now. You're used."

And I believed it. So easily. Because I had already been living with the false belief that if my own father didn't want me, how could anyone else?

I wrapped that trauma in another lie:

"I just see the good in people."

"I always try to understand where people are coming from."

And the most dangerous one:

"Maybe it wasn't that bad."

I gave grace to people who didn't deserve it. Repeatedly. I mistook self-abandonment for compassion. I let others hurt me if it meant they wouldn't leave. Because deep down, I thought that was the price of love.

It wasn't until I started therapy in 2021 that the walls began to crack. For the first time, I had someone reflect the truth back to me – not the watered-down version I had convinced myself was noble, but the *real* truth. My therapist helped me see that grace is beautiful, but not everyone deserves equal access to it. He reminded me that I can still be a good person, even if I stop pretending that *everyone else* is.

That it's okay to stop lying.

That it's okay to stop surviving.

That healing starts when we start telling the truth
— to ourselves first.

I spent years protecting the people who hurt me — until I realized I was the one bleeding.

Chapter 5:

When I Became a Mother

They say becoming a parent teaches you everything you didn't know you needed to heal. They're right.

When I became a mother - at 20 years old, something in me shifted. Not immediately – but slowly, and all at once. The moment I held my son in my arms, I felt the weight of every generation before me… and the power to do something different.

I looked at him and saw the start of something new – something I never had. Not just love, but *safe* love. Unconditional, nurturing, consistent love. I didn't want to just protect him from the world. I wanted to protect him from the kind of wounds I still carried. The ones that weren't visible but deeply embedded.

I didn't have the perfect blueprint. I wasn't handed a roadmap. But I knew exactly what I didn't want to repeat. I wasn't going to make my son feel small to keep someone else comfortable. I wasn't going to teach him that love was something you earn, or that affection is only given when you're easy to handle.

I was going to do it differently.

Because I remember what it felt like to be silenced. To be invisible. To cry alone in my room, wondering what I did wrong. To apologize too loudly, feeling too much, needing too often.

I swore he would never have to wonder if he was loved. I'd tell him a thousand times a day. I'd show him in the way I listened, in the way I held him, in the way I'd never make him feel like he had to be perfect to be worthy.

Motherhood wasn't just a title – it was my revolution. The beginning of breaking generational cycles that had long gone unspoken. I didn't want to parent from my pain. I wanted to parent from my healing.

Growing up, discipline meant punishment. It meant silence, grounding, and isolation. It meant being shut out instead of being heard. And over time, I learned that expressing emotion only brought consequences – not comfort.

I knew I wanted something different for my son.

I want him to know that having big feelings doesn't make him bad. That tears aren't a weakness. That frustration, sadness, and anger are all allowed – and that he doesn't have to hide those feelings to be loved.

When he's overwhelmed, I don't send him away. I sit with him. I breathe with him. I teach him that emotions are not something to fear or suppress, but something to move *through* together.

I don't always get it perfect – but I always come back. I repair. I reconnect. Because that's what I needed as a child and rarely received.

Discipline in our home doesn't mean punishment. It means guidance. It means safety. It means showing him that I'm a soft place to land, even when the world – or his own body – feels too big.

I'm not just raising my son. I'm re-raising myself in the process.

And every time I choose connection over control, love over shame, presence over power – I heal a little more of the girl I used to be. The one who sat quietly in her room, wondering why no one came to check if she was okay.

The cycle ends with me.

Daddy Where Are You?

(Written October 2015, Age 14)

Daddy, where are you?
I've been waiting
for the day you come home.

I think I'm over-dreaming—
because this dream
is turning into a nightmare.

All those dreams I had,
of having a dad
who truly cares about me…
Where have you been?

You've missed me growing up.
You've missed most of my life.

Half of my heart wants to love you.
The other half says no.

If only you understood
what it feels like to be alone—
to wonder:
Is he ever coming home?

My dreams have ended.
They've turned into nightmares.

Which means…
if you truly miss me,
come find me.

If you don't—
just stay away.

I have nothing left to say.
No more tears
to bring you back around.

I'm done.
I must live my life.

Come, Daddy—
I will show you the way
back into my heart.

It's you who decides
whether to follow the path
or stay behind.

To you, I give the full power.
It's your decision.
I just hope you make the right one.

This was the last time she begged.

After this, she stopped asking him to come back.

Chapter 6:

The Final Straw: Going No Contact

There comes a point where the damage stops being a memory and becomes a pattern. A loop. A slow bleed you either learn to live with – or finally choose to stop.

For most of my life, I kept trying with my father. I clung to the idea that maybe this time would be different. That if I could just word things the right way, stay calm enough, be patient enough, maybe he'd finally hear me.

He never did.

What I've come to realize is that narcissists don't lack the ability to understand – they lack the willingness. My father couldn't take accountability for anything that reflected poorly on him. If I expressed hurt, it was "disrespect." If I asked for change, I was "blaming." If I set a boundary, I was being "ungrateful."

I've re-read messages more times than I can count – the ones I shared with him during some of our final conversations. Calm. Direct. Honest. And still, his responses always circled back to the same thing: **deflection.** He refused to even consider the possibility that he had hurt me.

"You're always so dramatic."

"I'm sorry you feel that way."

"You're trying to rewrite the past."

No matter how gently I approached him, it always ended the same: with me feeling like I was the one who did something wrong.

But the final straw came in the form of a blow-up. It came in the form of quiet, exhausted knowing. A moment where I realized: **he's not going to change.** And if I keep letting him in, I'll keep bleeding for someone who won't even acknowledge the wound.

I didn't go no contact out of anger – I did it out of necessity.

It was always the same pattern.

I'd express something calmly – some hurt, some hope – and it would unravel into a defense session. No matter how softly I said it, how carefully I worded it, how many disclaimers I wrapped around my feelings… he'd twist it.

"You need to stop blaming everyone for your problems."

"I never said that. You're remembering it wrong."

"I did the best I could. Sorry it wasn't enough for you."

Every time I tried to hold up a mirror, he shattered it. Every boundary became an argument. Every attempt at honestly became a personal attack — to him. Not once did he sit with my pain. Not once did he say, *"Tell me what I did so I can understand."* It was never about listening. It was about maintaining his image.

And for a long time, I still clung to hope. I'd tell myself, *maybe this time he'll hear me. Maybe this time, he'll realize I'm not trying to fight – I'm just trying to be heard.*

But narcissists don't respond to truth. They respond to control.

The last conversation we had wasn't explosive – it was exhausting. I remember reading his words and feeling nothing but emptiness. I had tried everything. I had bent over backward to create peace. And still, he couldn't admit even one thing he had done wrong.

That's when it clicked.

He was never going to meet me where I was. Not because I was unreachable – but because he was never willing to come down off his pedestal. He wanted the version of me that smiled and stayed silent. And that version of me no longer existed.

So, I stopped answering.

I didn't block him in anger – I just chose silence. Peace. I told myself that I didn't need a dramatic ending to justify my departure. The slow, steady erosion of trust was enough. I had every right to leave a relationship that left me feeling more hurt than held.

But it wasn't easy.

I didn't realize this until my therapist asked me a seemingly simple question:

"If this were anyone else, would you be letting them treat you like this?"

"Family doesn't get a free pass to be hurtful or disrespectful just because they're blood."

There was guilt. So much guilt. Because no matter how broken the relationship was, he was still my father. And part of me still carried the ache of that little girl, standing by the door, waiting for her dad to show up.

I mourned the father I never had more than the one I left behind.

But with distance came clarity. I stopped second-guessing myself. I stopped rewriting conversations in my head, wondering what I could've said differently. I stopped shrinking to keep the peace in a war that wasn't mine to fight anymore.

And slowly, I started to feel free.

I began focusing on the people who *did* show up for me. The family *I* was building. The husband who loved me without conditions. The son who would never have to wonder if his emotions were too much.

Walking away didn't mean I gave up. It meant I chose to stop bleeding for someone who never brought a bandage.

I didn't go no contact because I hated him – I did it because I finally loved myself more. He didn't lose me all at once. He lost me every time he chose pride over love. And in the end, I didn't need him to change. I just needed him out of the way of my healing.

Part II:

The Healing (Self-Help + Reflection)

Chapter 7:

What Narcissistic Abuse REALLY Looks Like

Narcissistic abuse doesn't always look like screaming, hitting, or name-calling.

Sometimes, it looks like silence.

Like being ignored when you're hurting.

Like being made to feel your needs are too much.

Like always feeling like *you* are the problem.

Narcissistic abuse is slow and subtle. It chips away at your self-worth over time. It confuses you. It makes you second-guess your reality. It teaches you to apologize for things that were never your fault.

Its *emotional manipulation* dressed up as "parenting," "love," or "help."

It's being told you're ungrateful when you express pain.

It's being given affection only when you're easy to love – and punished when you're not.

For years, I didn't realize what I had lived through *had* a name. I just thought I was dramatic. Difficult. Too sensitive.

But the more I learned, the more I realized – I wasn't broken. I had been conditioned to believe I was.

If you've ever:

- Felt invisible in your own family
- Been guilted for setting boundaries
- Questioned your memory because someone kept rewriting your truth
- Apologized just to keep the peace, even when you did nothing wrong
- Been told you were "too much," "too emotional," or "always playing the victim" …

You may have experienced narcissistic abuse.

And it you have – *I see you*. I know how isolating it feels. How long it takes to even say those words out loud. But naming it is the first step toward healing.

Narcissistic abuse doesn't always leave bruises. It leaves confusion. Self-doubt. Anxiety. Guilt.

Here are just a few of the ways it shows up:

Emotional Patterns and Behaviors of Narcissistic Abuse:

You constantly feel like you're walking on eggshells.

You learn to tiptoe around someone's moods, their reactions, their silence. You adjust *everything* to avoid upsetting them – because even the smallest things can become a blow-up.

You're gaslit into doubting your own memory or feelings.

"I never said that."

"You're making things up."

"You're too sensitive."

Over time, you stop trusting yourself.

Affection is used as a reward

Love, attention, and validation are only given when you're behaving the way they want. The moment you express pain or push back? The warmth disappears.

You're made to feel guilty for having boundaries

If you try to set limits, they flip it: "You're being selfish." "You're cutting me out." "You don't care about family."

Suddenly, you're the bad guy – for protecting your peace.

You're blamed for things that were never yours to carry.

If they hurt you, it's because *you made them angry.*

If you're upset, you're "being dramatic"

They are never the problem – you always are.

They weaponize your empathy

They know you'll feel guilty. They know you'll try to see the good. And the use that – again and again – to keep you tied to them.

They rewrite your story

Even if you have the proof – screenshots, receipts, memories – they'll say it never happened that way. And when no one backs you up? You start to wonder… if maybe they're right.

At some point, you start to shrink. You edit yourself. You apologize for your emotions. You become so focused on keeping the peace, you forget what it feels like to be whole.

But here's the truth:

You were never too much. You were never the problem. You were just trying to survive in an environment that punished you for being human.

Reflection: Could This Be You?

Take a moment. Answer Honestly – there are no right or wrong responses here. There are simply to help you see clearly.

1. Do I often second-guess myself, even in situations where I used to feel confident?
2. Have I ever apologized just to "keep the peace," even when I didn't do anything wrong?
3. Do I feel anxious before interacting with a specific person, worried about how they'll react?
4. Have I been told I'm too emotional, too dramatic, or too sensitive – especially when I try to express pain?
5. Do I ever feel like I need to *earn* someone's love or attention by being "good"?
6. When I try to talk about past hurt, am I made to feel guilty or crazy?
7. Do I feel drained, confused, or not like myself after certain conversations?

If you answered "yes" to any of these… you're not alone. You're not broken. And you're *not* imagining it.

Tools for Healing:

Journal Prompt:

What are some "truths" I've been told about myself that may not actually be true?

Grounding Reminder:

You are allowed to take up space.

You are allowed to have feelings.

You are allowed to be safe in your relationships.

Affirmations:

My emotions are valid, even if others try to dismiss them.

I do not owe anyone access to me just because we share blood.

I can rewrite the story. I am not who they said I was.

For me, the moment of realization wasn't dramatic. It wasn't a blow-up. It was quiet. Almost anticlimactic.

I had just reread a conversation with my father – one of those long message threads where I tried so hard to express myself. To explain the impact his behavior had on me. I was calm, respectful, vulnerable.

And yet, his response was the same as always: deflection, denial, defensiveness. He didn't acknowledge my pain – he turned it back on me.

"I never said that."

"You're remembering it wrong."

"I'm sorry you feel that way, but that's not what happened."

I stared at the screen and felt this wave of…nothing. Just clarity. Not sadness. Not anger. Just the full-body understanding that **he was never going to change –** and that I had been rewriting myself to make his version of love seem livable.

That was the moment I saw it clearly:

This wasn't miscommunication. This was emotional manipulation. This wasn't a tough relationship. This was abuse.

It didn't matter how hard I tried. It didn't matter how careful I was. He was never going to validate my truth – because doing so would mean admitting his part in the pain.

And I finally stopped trying to convince him.

That's what narcissistic abuse really looks like.

It looks like silence. Gaslighting. Emotional withdrawal. It looks like never been enough, no matter how hard you try.

But most of all – it looks like waking up one day and deciding: **I deserve better than this.**

Clarity doesn't scream. It whispers, **"You don't have to live like this."**

Chapter 8:

Boundaries Are Not Betrayal

For most of my life, I believed that saying "no" made me a bad person.

That standing up for myself meant I was being ungrateful. That asking for space was an act of war. That creating boundaries meant I was pushing people away.

But the truth is, boundaries are not walls – they are bridges to peace.

Boundaries are how we protect our energy, our hearts, and our healing. They are not punishments. They are not ultimatums. They are simply the language of *self-respect*.

But when you grow up in dysfunction – especially around narcissistic people – you're taught that boundaries are betrayal. That you're being difficult.

That you're "cutting people off" just for having expectations. And slowly, you start to believe it.

I can't tell you how many times I felt guilty just for asking someone not to speak to me a certain way. For asking for space. For pulling back when the relationship became unsafe.

I was told I was being dramatic. That I was starting unnecessary conflict. That I was cold, rude, or "not the same girl I used to be."

And maybe I wasn't. Maybe I was finally becoming the woman I was always meant to be – the one who no longer sacrifices her peace to keep the people around her comfortable.

Because the truth is: **you are not required to stay small just to make others feel big.**

I remember the first time I truly set a boundary with my father.

It wasn't aggressive. It wasn't yelling. I was simply asking him to acknowledge how his actions had hurt me. I said it calmly, with love – even with hope. But instead of hearing me, he reacted with anger.

"I'm tired of always being blamed."

"You're just trying to rewrite the past."

"You should be grateful I did anything at all."

That was the moment I realized – some people don't want peace. They want control. And when you stop allowing it, they call *you* the problem.

I've set boundaries with others too – family members who made me feel small, people who treated my kindness like currency they could cash in whenever they wanted. And each time, I was met with resistance. With guilt-trips. With silence.

"Why are you acting like this?"

"You're not the same person anymore."

"You've changed."

Yes. I have changed.

Because healing *does* that. It rewires you. It teaches you that love doesn't mean self-abandonment. That protecting your peace isn't selfish – it's sacred.

Learning to set boundaries without guilt.

Boundaries felt unnatural at first. They felt like confrontation. Like disconnection. Like I was being "mean." I had spent so long managing other people's emotions that I thought I had to explain every choice, soften every "no," justify every limit.

But the truth is: **you don't have to explain why you're protecting yourself.**

Boundaries are not about shutting people out. They are about letting the right people in. They are the gatekeepers of peace.

I started small. I said, *"I'm not available for this conversation right now."*

I said, *"I love you, but I won't continue this discussion if it turns hurtful."*

And every time I honored my boundaries; I felt a piece of myself return.

How comfortable are you with boundaries?

1. When someone hurts you, do you speak up or stay silent to keep the peace?
2. Do you feel responsible for how other people react to your boundaries?
3. Have you ever been called "difficult," "too sensitive," or "dramatic" after expressing a need?
4. Do you struggle to say "no" even when you feel overwhelmed or drained?
5. Do you explain or defend your choices even when they're valid?
6. Who in your life respects your boundaries — and who pushes them?

Remember: the way people react to your boundaries tells you everything about the relationship — not about your worth.

Boundary Scripts for Real Life:

You don't need to be aggressive to be clear. You just need to be honest and grounded.

Here are a few phrases that can help:

- *"I'm not comfortable discussing that."*
- *"I understand that's your opinion, but I'm choosing something different for myself."*
- *"That feels hurtful to me. If we are going to continue this conversation, it needs to be respectful."*
- *"I won't be responding to messages that are manipulative or guilt driven."*
- *"It's okay if you don't agree, but this is what I need."*

You are not responsible for making others comfortable at the cost of your own well-being.

Boundaries can protect peace without destroying connection.

For a long time, I thought that was just the price of keeping the peace – let the comments slide, let the questions go unanswered, smile politely and change the subject. But I've learned that silence doesn't protect peace – it just delays the conflict. And sometimes, it quietly erodes you in the process.

Not long ago, my grandma – my father's mother – brought up my decision to go no contact with him. Again. She's always wanted to "fix" things between us. And while I know her intentions weren't malicious; they were still invasive.

That day, I told her gently but clearly: *"This is between me and him. I'm not comfortable talking about it."*

She pushed.

"Well, I want to talk about it."

"He misses you. He's a good person."

Then she mentioned something I had only ever shared in a private email to my father.

She said, *"So he just has to go to therapy and everything will be fine?"*

It wasn't just the breech of privacy that hurt – it was the realization that my boundaries were being discussed, judged, and misunderstood by people who weren't even part of the conversation. I responded calmly:

"No, therapy isn't a magic fix. But it's a start. He knows what the conditions are. It's up to him to meet them – not anyone else."

After that visit, I sent her a message. I told her honestly that the conversation made me uncomfortable. That my boundaries were not respected. That I was willing to maintain our relationship – just like we had my whole life without my father's involvement – but I wouldn't continue visiting if the topic of my father was going to be brought up again, especially in front of my son.

To her credit, she responded with grace. She apologized. She said she understood, and that it was "the mom in her" that wanted to fix things. And as a mother now, I get that. I really do.

I also wonder if part of her sees the truth — what her son has become — but just can't fully bring herself to name it. I don't blame her. If it were my child, it would break me too.

Our next visit? It was one of the best we've had in months. No tension. No poking. No pushing. Just mutual respect and space for love.

That's the truth about boundaries: **when held with clarity and care, they don't destroy relationships — they refine them. They reveal which ones are rooted in control… and which ones are rooted in love.**

Respect doesn't fear boundaries. It honors them.

Chapter 9:

Learning to Reparent Myself

No one teaches you how to become your own parent.

You just wake up one day and realize: *no one is coming to save you.*

No one is going to give you the apology you deserved. No one is going to fill the hole left by the love you didn't get.

And so, you begin the quiet, sacred work of learning to give it to yourself.

That's what reparenting is.

It's not about blaming your parents forever – it's about understanding the *impact* they had and choosing to respond to your own wounds with love instead of shame.

It's saying to your inner child, *"I see you now. And I will never leave you behind again."*

Reparenting didn't start with some grand moment of awakening.

It started in a therapist's office – me sitting on a couch, unsure of what I even needed, but knowing deep down that something had to change.

Therapy helped med see the person I *really* was – not the version I had been told I was.

Not the "too much" girl.

Not the "difficult" daughter.

Not the "dramatic" woman who was "just looking for attention."

I stopped letting others define me by their inability to love me.

And for the first time, I started to get to know myself – not through someone else's lens, but my own. I started listening to the quiet voice inside that said, *"You are good. You are kind. You are worthy."*

One of the biggest things therapy gave me was this: **permission to feel.**

My therapist would say, *"That makes sense."*

Or *"Of course you feel that way."*

Simple words – but they rewired something in me.

I had spent so long believing I was *wrong* for feeling – too emotional, too sensitive, too reactive. But feelings aren't flaws. **They're human.**

Now, when I feel overwhelmed or triggered, I try to pause and say:

"It's okay to feel this way. You're not wrong. You're responding to something real."

That's reparenting.

It's not perfect. It's not always graceful. But it's the most loving thing I've ever done for myself.

Breaking the cycle of negative self-talk.

This one is still a work in progress.

For years, I joked about myself – casually.

"Of course I'd mess that up."

"Classic me."

"I'm such a mess."

It felt harmless. Light. Even funny sometimes. But the more I said it, the more I started to believe it.

Our minds are always listening.

Even when we're joking.

Now I try to catch myself. I ask:

"Would I say this to my son?" or "Would I want my son to say this about himself?"

Reparenting means showing yourself the same kindness, patience, and protection you would give to a child you loved deeply.

Reparenting didn't happen all at once. It happened slowly – in therapy sessions, in quiet moments of reflection, in the way I started to speak to myself when no one else was listening.

Therapy was the turning point.

It gave me a safe place to unravel. To feel without being judged. To say things out loud that I had carried silently for years.

It helped me stop defining myself by the versions of me that other people created.

I started to let go of those voices.

And I started to *listen to my own.*

My therapist told me something that changed everything:

"You're allowed to feel that."

Simple words – but no one had ever said them to me before. I had always been punished for feelings, not comforted. I had never been told that emotions were human. Natural. Acceptable.

So, I began practicing something radical: **emotional validation.**

Not from others — *from myself.*

I'd feel sadness, and instead of pushing it away, I'd say: *"Of course you feel this way. This makes sense."*

I'd feel anger, and instead of guilt, I'd say: *"You're allowed to be upset. You're not wrong for feeling hurt."*

I'm still unlearning the negative self-talk.

Sometimes it shows up like sarcasm or jokes — *"Well, I'm a mess,"* or *"Of course I screwed that up."*

But even in those little comments, I can hear the undertone: **you're still not enough.**

That's the voice I'm learning to challenge.

Not with shame.

But with softness.

With questions like: *Is that true? Would I speak to my younger self that way?*

Dear younger me,

I'm sorry that no one showed up for you the way you needed.

I'm sorry they made you feel like your emotions were a burden.

Like your voice didn't matter.

Like you had to earn love by being quiet, perfect, or easy to deal with.

You didn't deserve that.

You were not too much.

You were just a child trying to be seen.

And I see you now.

I promise to never abandon you again.

I promise to listen.

To comfort.

To love you without conditions.

From now on, I will be the adult you always needed.

Love,

Me

Reflection Questions:

Reconnecting With the Child Within

1. What did I need most as a child that I didn't receive?
2. When I feel triggered or emotional now, what age does that version of me feel like?
3. How can I show up for that younger version of myself with compassion?
4. What are some things I say to myself today that mimic the voices of others?
5. What new voice do I want to replace those old messaged with?

Affirmations for Reparenting & Self-Compassion:

- *My feelings are valid, even when they're messy.*
- *I don't have to earn love by being easy to handle.*
- *I can rewrite the way I speak to myself.*
- *It's okay to be a work in progress.*
- *I'm no longer waiting to be saved – I'm learning how to hold myself.*

She didn't need to be fixed. She just needed to be heard —
and I'm finally listening.

I am the safety she once searched for.

Chapter 10:

Anger, Grief, and the Guilt We Don't Deserve

For a long time, I didn't let myself feel angry.

I thought anger made me ungrateful. Or immature. Or cruel.

I didn't let myself grieve, either. Because how do you grieve someone who's still alive?

And the guilt? That was the one I knew best. The constant, quiet ache of wondering if maybe all of this was my fault. If I was just too emotional. Too difficult. Too hard to love.

The truth is, we are often taught that our pain is a problem. That feeling things too deeply means we're dramatic. Or broken. Or a burden. Especially when that pain comes from family.

But healing isn't possible without honesty.

And the honest truth is I *am* angry.

I *do* grieve.

And I'm done carrying guilt that was never mine to hold.

No one teaches daughters how to be angry safely. Especially not daughters of narcissistic fathers.

We're taught to be quiet. Grateful. Forgiving. We're taught to make peace, even when we're the ones bleeding.

But underneath that silence, there's rage.

Not the kind that lashes out – but the kind that simmers. The kind that builds up over years of being dismissed, minimized, gaslit, and ignored.

I'm angry that I spent so many years begging for scraps of love.

I'm angry that I was told I was the problem – when I was just a child trying to be seen.

I'm angry that I still hesitate to speak up, even now, because of how often I was punished for using my voice.

And you know what?

I'm allowed to be.

Because anger is not the opposite of healing – it's part of it.

Anger is what told me: *This isn't okay.*

It's what gave me the courage to set boundaries. To walk away. To stop letting people confuse love with control.

My anger wasn't dangerous. It was *informative.*

And for the first time, I'm not afraid to feel it.

The grief that no one talks about.

There's a kind of grief that doesn't come from death – it comes from absence. From longing for something that was never there in the first place.

I've grieved the father I wish I had.

The one who would have shown up. Listened. Protected me.

The one who would've cheered at my choir concerts. Been proud of my archery trophies. The one who would've remembered my favorite songs or knew what I liked.

I've grieved the childhood I never got to live.

The one where I wasn't walking on eggshells. The one where I didn't feel like a burden. The one where I was being hugged instead of hushed.

This kind of grief is complicated.

It doesn't follow the rules.

It shows up at random – at baby showers, during the holidays, in the middle of laughing with your child – and reminds you of all the things you missed.

And for a long time, I told myself it wasn't real grief.

Because *he's still alive*. Because *it could've been worse*.

But those are lies I told to avoid the deeper truth:

I lost something.

And that loss deserves to be mourned.

Grief isn't just about letting go of someone.

Sometimes, it's about letting go of the hope that they'll ever become who you needed them to be.

The Guilt We Don't Deserve

Guilt was the heaviest thing I ever carried.

Heavier than anger. Heavier than grief.

Because guilt doesn't just weigh you down — it convinces you that the weight belongs to you.

I felt guilty for going no contact.

Guilty for setting boundaries.

Guilty for not trying harder, not reaching out, not being "the bigger person."

I even felt guilty for being hurt.

"He did the best he could."

"He's still your father."

"At least he was around sometimes…"

Every time I tried to name my pain; guilt came in to shut the door.

But guilt isn't always a sign you did something wrong.

Sometimes, it's a sign you're finally doing something *different*.

Because here's the truth:

- You're not selfish for walking away from someone who hurts you — even if they're family.
- You're not ungrateful for protecting your peace.

- You're not a bad daughter for no longer being the *only* one trying.
- You're not the villain for refusing to carry the dysfunction forward.

You didn't cause the damage.

But you are allowed to stop the bleeding.

And that doesn't make you cruel.

That makes you *free*.

A Permission Slip for the Wounded Heart:

You are allowed to feel your anger.

You are allowed to grieve what was never given.

You are allowed to stop carrying guilt that doesn't belong to you.

This is your permission slip to:

- Say *no* without explanation
- Protect your peace unapologetically
- Greive someone who's still alive.
- Be angry about what happened – and about what didn't
- Stop trying to fix people who refuse to meet you halfway

- Choose yourself, even when it disappoints others.

You don't owe anyone comfort at the expense of your own healing.

You are allowed to be soft and fierce.

You are allowed to tell the truth – even when it makes others uncomfortable.

Most of all:

You are allowed to heal. Fully. Freely. Loudly, if you want. Silently, if you need. On your own terms.

Reflection Prompts: Releasing the Weight

1. What emotion have I been taught to suppress or ignore? Why?
2. When do I feel most guilty – and does that guilt belong to me, or someone else's expectations?
3. What grief am I still carrying that I haven't fully acknowledged?
4. What would it look like to give myself permission to feel, without judgment?
5. If I could speak to the part of me that still feels responsible for everything... what would I say?

Feeling it all isn't weakness – it's healing. And I'm allowed to feel without apology.

Grief made me human. Anger made me brave. Releasing guilt made me free.

Chapter 11:

Becoming the Parent I Needed

I didn't just become a mom – I became the parent I always needed.

The one who listens.

The one who holds space.

The one who never makes love feel conditional.

I used to think breaking cycles would feel loud, dramatic – like some kind of rebellion. But instead, it looks like small, intentional moments. The quiet pauses before reacting. The deep breaths before responding. The choice to lean in instead of shutting down.

It looks like sitting beside my son when he's overwhelmed instead of sending him away.

It looks like telling him, *"I know it's hard right now. I'm here."*

It looks like letting him cry without rushing to fix it. Letting him feel without being told to stop. Letting him be angry without calling it disrespect.

Every time I do that; I'm not just parenting him.

I'm reparenting *me*.

Because I remember what it felt like to be punished for being emotional.

To be labeled "dramatic" or "difficult" when I was just hurting.

To be grounded instead of comforted. Ignored instead of understood.

I didn't want my son to grow up having to recover from my parenting.

So, I chose differently.

And that choice heals me every day.

One of the biggest shifts in my parenting has been this:

I don't punish my son for struggling.

I don't punish him for having big feelings. I don't take love away when he's overwhelmed. I don't confuse discipline with disconnection.

Because I remember what it felt like to be grounded every weekend, not for being cruel or reckless – but for being emotional.

For talking back when I felt unheard.

For crying "too much."

For reacting like a child – because I *was* a child.

So now, when my son is having a hard time, I choose connection first.

I get down on his level. I look him in the eyes. I say,

"It's okay to feel this way. I'm here. Let's work through it together."

Not because I'm perfect. Not because I never get frustrated.

But because I've learned that healing doesn't come from silence or shame – it comes from being seen.

Every time I break the pattern of yelling, or punishing, or pulling away –

Every time I choose empathy over ego –

Every time I show up with love instead of control –

I'm becoming the parent I needed.

Parenting From Healing, Not Hurt

This is what it means to parent from healing:

- I pause before I react
- I apologize when I get it wrong
- I listen to understand, not to correct
- I create safety, not fear

I don't need my son to be "easy."

I need him to feel safe enough to be *honest*.

Because that's the kind of child I was – and the kind I wasn't allowed to be.

Reflection: For Parents Breaking the Cycle:

1. What did I need most as a child that I can now give to my own child?
2. How did the adults in my life respond when I was upset, scared, or angry?
3. When I feel triggered as a parent, is it about the moment in front of me – or the past behind me?
4. What do I want my child to remember about how I made them feel?
5. Can I allow space for both: to be a work in progress and a safe parent?

Every time I choose connection over control; I give my child — and my younger self — a new ending.

Chapter 12:

Finding Peace Without Closure

I used to believe that healing required closure.

That peace could only come once I had answers. Once I had an apology. Once the people who hurt me finally understood the damage they caused.

But I've learned that closure doesn't always come from a conversation.

Sometimes, it comes from a decision.

A quiet one.

A heavy one.

But still – a choice.

Because the truth is, there are people who will never take accountability.

There are wounds that will never be acknowledged.

There are stories that will never be told the way they actually happened – at least not by the ones who cause them.

And I've stopped waiting.

I've stopped waiting for my father to say, "I'm sorry."

I've stopped hoping for the moment where he realizes what he lost.

I've stopped needing him to finally see me – because I see myself now.

And that is enough.

Letting go without closure didn't happen all at once.

There wasn't a final conversation that tied everything up neatly.

There was no dramatic ending. No resolution. No confession.

Just me… realizing that the silence wasn't going to break, and the truth wasn't going to be recognized.

And still – I chose to move forward.

I let go the day I stopped checking my messages for a response.

The day I stopped rehearsing how I'd explain it all if he ever asked.

The day I stopped needing him to understand and started needing *myself* to feel free.

That kind of peace is quieter than I expected.

It doesn't shout. It doesn't feel like victory.

It feels like exhaling.

Like finally being able to put the weight down.

And with that release came a kind of softness I hadn't felt in years.

I stopped carrying the armor.

Stopped rewriting the story to make it less painful.

Stopped begging for something that was never mine to begin with: his accountability.

Instead, I started listening to my own truth – uninterrupted.

"He hurt me."

"He chose not to show up."

"I deserved better."

And then I added the sentence that changed everything.

"I don't need him to say it for it to be true."

Journal Prompt:

What have I been waiting to hear? And if that apology never comes…, can I still release it?

A Personal Release Ritual:

Write a letter to the person that hurt you — not to send, but to say everything they never gave you space to say.

Then write a second letter to yourself.

Tell yourself what you needed to hear.

Validate the pain.

Affirm the strength.

End it with:

"I release the need for closure from them. I choose peace, for me."

Daily Reminder:

"Their silence is not my responsibility. Their denial is not my truth."

He may never own what he did, but I no longer carry it.

Part III:

The Becoming

Chapter 13:

Reclaiming Joy

For a long time, I didn't trust joy.

It felt too temporary. Too fragile. Like if I let myself get too comfortable in it, it would be taken from me – just like everything else.

When you've spent years surviving, joy doesn't come naturally.

You learn to brace yourself instead.

To wait for the other shoe to drop.

To expect loss before you ever allow love to land.

But healing taught me something else:

Joy isn't a reward for finally being okay.

It's part of what make us okay.

Reclaiming joy was about giving myself permission to feel good without guilt.

To laugh loudly.

To dance with my son in the kitchen.

To sing along to music in the car with the windows down.

To rest without apologizing.

To feel light in my chest, even when the world still holds heavy things.

Because joy isn't the absence of pain – it's the reminder that pain doesn't get to have the final word.

It didn't happen all at once.

Joy didn't return with fanfare.

It came in quietly – soft moments that felt small but stayed with me.

Like hearing my son belly laugh for the first time and realizing I didn't feel numb – I felt *warm*.

Like catching myself smiling in the mirror – not out of obligation, but because I meant it.

Like sitting outside with a cup of coffee and realizing I didn't have to be doing anything to be at peace.

It was joy in the ordinary.

Joy in *not* explaining myself.

Joy in healing, not because I had to – but because I wanted to live differently.

And more than anything, it was the joy of showing my child what freedom feels like.

Letting him run barefoot in the grass.

Letting him make a mess and laugh through it.

Letting him be fully, unapologetically himself.

It's not always loud. It's not always easy.

But every time I choose presence over perfection; I reclaim another piece of myself.

What Joy Looks Like Now

Joy used to feel distant – something reserved for "better" people with easier lives.

Now I know better.

Joy looks like boundaries without guilt.

Like choosing softness without feeling weak.

Like resting without needing to earn it.

Like loving myself – even when the healing is still messy.

Joy doesn't mean I'm done grieving.

It means I've made room for *both*.

I still carry pain – but it doesn't carry me anymore.

Prompts: Returning to Joy:

1. When was the last time I felt real joy – no matter how small the moment?
2. What does joy look like for me now that I'm no longer surviving?
3. What old beliefs tell me I'm not allowed to feel good?
4. What would it mean to choose joy anyway?
5. If I could create a joy ritual – a small act that brings light into my day – what would it be?

I found joy in the places that once held grief – and I let it stay.

Chapter 14:

Love That Doesn't Hurt

I didn't know what love was supposed to feel like.

I only knew the kind that made me question myself.

The kind that asked me to shrink.

The kind that kept score.

The kind that hurt – but called itself love anyway.

So, when I finally experienced love that didn't hurt, I didn't trust it at first.

I waited for the other shoe to drop.

For the disappointment.

For the moment where I'd be told I was too much again.

But it never came.

Because this time, love looked different.

It didn't explode – it stayed,

It didn't silence – it listened.

It didn't ask me to earn it – it gave itself freely.

Real love – the kind that doesn't hurt – felt foreign at first.

It was quiet.

It didn't demand.

It didn't weaponize my emotions.

It didn't disappear when things got hard.

When I met my husband, I didn't fully know how to receive the kind of love he offered.

Gentle. Patient. Steady.

The kind that didn't raise its voice.

The kind that didn't use silence as a punishment.

The kind that stayed beside me even when I was messy or unsure.

He didn't love me for who he wanted me to be – he loved me for exactly who I was.

Even the parts I thought were unlovable.

Even the parts I was still healing.

And slowly, I started to believe it was real.

Learning to Receive Love:

It wasn't easy at first.

When you're only known love that came with conditions, you start to believe that's all love ever is.

You expect to be abandoned. You expect to be questioned. You expect that the moment you ask for too much – you'll lose it.

But he didn't leave.

He didn't punish me for needing reassurance.

He didn't throw my past in my face when I got triggered.

He didn't ask me to apologize for having baggage.

Instead, he created space for me to unpack it safely.

And he stayed.

That's what real love looks like:

Not perfection. Not constant sunshine.

But **safety. Kindness. Choice.**

Love isn't supposed to confuse you.

It's not supposed to make you smaller.

It's not supposed to feel like survival.

Reflection: What Love Feels Like Now:

1. What did love look like growing up – and how did it shape what I expected from others?
2. What beliefs do I still carry about being "too much" to love?
3. How does it feel to be loved without conditions?
4. What's one thing I've learned from being loved in a healthy way?
5. What kind of love am I choosing to model for my child?

Real love stayed when my fears showed up. He didn't fix me.
He loved me while I fixed myself.

Chapter 15:

The Inner Critic vs. The Inner Child

For most of my life, I lived with a voice in my head that wasn't mine.

It told me I was too sensitive.

Too emotional.

Too dramatic.

Too much.

It sounded like my father. Like my stepmother. Like every adult who ever punished me for feeling too deeply.

That voice wasn't just cruel – it was *constant*.

It made me doubt myself before I even spoke.

It made me shrink in rooms where I should've been seen.

It made me afraid to be wrong, afraid to take up space, afraid to believe I was enough.

That voice became my inner critic.

And for a long time, I thought it was me.

But then I started healing.

And I realized there was another voice buried underneath the noise.

It was quieter. Softer.

It said things like:

"You're doing your best."

"You didn't deserve that."

"You're allowed to rest."

That voice?

That was my inner child.

The part of me that had been ignored for so long – finally learning how to speak.

Even now, the inner critic still shows up.

Not always as a scream – sometimes just a whisper.

"You're being too emotional again."

"They're not going to take you seriously."

"You're not doing enough."

Sometimes it even wears a disguise. It shows up as a joke —

"Of course I messed that up."

"I'm a disaster."

But the truth is: *that voice was never mine to begin with.*

It was shaped by the people who didn't know how to love me gently.

It was molded by year of emotional silence, by expectations I could never meet, by punishments I didn't deserve.

And slowly, I'm learning to respond differently.

Not with shame.

But with compassion.

Giving the Mic Back to My Inner Child:

When I notice that voice creeping in, I pause.

I picture my younger self — quiet, uncertain, trying so hard to be "good."

And I ask myself:

Would I say this to her?

Would I let someone speak to her this way?

The answer is always no.

So instead, I speak back with softness.

"You're safe now."

"You don't have to be perfect."

"You're not too much — you were never too much."

I've learned that the inner child doesn't need to be silenced — she needs to be heard.

And the inner critic?

She doesn't need to be hated.

She needs to be retrained.

Because even that voice came from survival.

But I'm not surviving anymore.

I'm healing.

I'm rewriting the script.

A Conversation Between the Critic, the Child, and Me:

Inner Critic:

You're too emotional. You always take things too personally. People won't take you seriously if you keep crying every time something hurts.

Inner Child:

But it really did hurt… I just wanted someone to understand.

Me (now):

I hear you both.

You – the critic – you were trying to protect me. You thought if I stayed quiet, small, or agreeable, I'd be safe. I see that now.

But I'm not that little girl anymore. I don't need protection through silence. I need permission to speak.

And you – the child – you've waited so long to be heard. You were never too much. You were *feeling* what no one would hold with you. I'm holding you now.

Reflection Prompt: Healing the Voice Within

1. What is one phrase my inner critic says that I no longer want to believe?
2. Where do I think that voice came from? Who taught it to me?
3. What does my inner child need to hear most today?
4. How can I create space for both voices – without letting the critic lead?

5. What would it feel like to let compassion speak louder than the shame?

I stopped letting the critic define me. I let the child guide me home.

Chapter 16:

You're Not Alone

For so long, I thought I was the only one.

I thought no one would understand the ache of being dismissed by your own parent.

The weight of constantly questioning your memories. The guilt of choosing peace over family.

I thought if I said it out loud – *"My father hurt me"* – people would look at me like I was the problem.

But then I started speaking.

First in therapy.

Then in quiet conversations with trusted friends.

Then in spaces created by survivors just like me.

And slowly, I realized: **I was never alone.**

There are so many of us – daughters, sons, partners, cycle-breakers – who grew up believing we were too much, too sensitive, too hard to love… only to learn later that we were simply responding to emotional neglect and manipulation.

The more I shared, the more I was met with:

"Me too."

"I thought it was just me."

"I've never said this out loud before, but…"

There's something deeply healing about being seen – *really seen* – without needing to explain yourself. About being in a space where your story is met with validation, not disbelief.

For me, the most important kind of support came through therapy.

Week after week, I sat across from someone who didn't just listen – he *believed me*. He validated my story. He reminded me that I wasn't crazy, and I wasn't too much. I was just someone who had been hurt, deeply, and was still learning how to live without shrinking.

Therapy gave me the language I needed.

Community gave me the *echo*.

I found online spaces -support groups, Facebook pages, mental health accounts – filled with people who had walked roads that looked a lot like mine.

Their stories sounded like mine. Their pain felt like mine. And for the first time, I didn't feel strange for needing to heal from something most people would never understand.

Because unless you've lived through emotional neglect or narcissistic abuse, it's hard to explain how *invisible* it makes you feel.

That's why community matters.

Not the kind that tells you to "forgive and forget," or "be the bigger person." But the kind that says, *"I see you. You're not broken. And you don't have to go back to be whole."*

If you're still in the part of your journey where you feel isolated, I want you to know this:

There are people out there who will understand you. You just haven't met them all yet.

- Start with therapy, if you're able. Not every therapist will be the right fit – but the right one can change your life.

- Look for online groups, survivor communities, or books written by people who get it.
- Reach out to a friend who listens without judgement – even one person who says *"me too"* can be the beginning of something bigger.

And if none of that feels safe yet… know that reading this book, writing your truth, even just *thinking* about healing, is a form of reaching out.

You are not alone in this.

A Message to You:

If you've made it this far, I want you to know something:

You are incredibly brave.

You've survived things no one saw. You've carried stores that others tried to silence. And now – you're still here. Still healing. Still becoming.

There's no perfect way to do this work. Some days you'll feel strong. Some days you'll still ache. But *you are not alone.*

You are not too much.

You are not broken.

You are not wrong fro protecting your peace.

And if no one ever told you this before –

I'm proud of you.

A Letter to My Son and Future Children:

My loves,

If you ever find yourselves feeling lost, unseen, or unsure of who you are – please come back to these words.

This book is more than a story. It's the journey I took to become the mother you know.

The one who listens. Who holds space. Who protects you fiercely.

The one who chooses softness. Who loves you freely.

The one who shows up.

I didn't always have that kind of love growing up.

I had to fight for it, even within myself.

But that fight made me strong. And that strength – it's yours now too.

If life ever makes you feel small, I want you to remember:

Youn are allowed to take up space.

You are allowed to feel everything.

You are allowed to choose peace, even if it means walking away from people who don't understand it.

And if you ever need to gather the strength to do something hard – look back at this.

Look at the woman I became.

Look at the cycles I broke.

I did it for me.

But more than that – I did it for *you*.

You will never have to recover from my love.

You will only rise from it.

And if the day ever comes when you need courage,

I hope you'll remember:

Mom did it.

And so can you.

With all my love,

Mom

A Final Note, From My Story to Yours:

Dear reader,

You've walked through a lot with me.

Some of it may have felt familiar. Some of it may have cracked something open.

And some of it may have reminded you of just how strong you really are.

This isn't just my story – it's *ours*.

Because healing doesn't happen in isolation.

It happens in community. In truth. In choosing ourselves repeatedly.

So, if you're still learning how to let go...

Still learning how to trust your voice...

Still trying to believe that your feelings matter –

Keep going.

You are not behind. You are not broken.

You are not defined by who couldn't love you the way you needed.

You are allowed to heal loudly.

You are allowed to heal quietly.

You are allowed to heal in *your own way*.

Thank you for holding my story.

Now go hold yours – with both hands and your whole heart.

You're not alone.

Love,

A fellow cycle breaker

About the Author

Genevieve is a writer, mother, and survivor who has turned her pain into purpose. After years of navigating the complex and often invisible wounds of narcissistic abuse, she began her healing journey not just for herself—but for her children, present and future.

Her writing is rooted in vulnerability, resilience, and hope. She believes in breaking generational cycles, parenting with intention, and creating a life filled with softness, boundaries, and truth. Her deepest passion is helping others feel seen, heard, and not alone.

When she's not writing, she's likely chasing joy in the everyday laughing with her son, spending time with her husband, or reflecting on how far she's come.

This is her first book.